ELITE PUTTING

A Strokes-Gained Approach
to Mastering the Greens

Brendon DeVore
with Philip Reed

Copyright © 2023 Brendon DeVore and Philip Reed

All rights reserved

No part of this book may be reproduced, or stored in a retrieval system, or transmitted in any form or by any means, electronic, mechanical, photocopying, recording, or otherwise, without express written permission of the publisher.

ISBN-13: 9781234567890
ISBN-10: 1477123456

Cover design by: Brendon DeVore
Library of Congress Control Number: 2018675309
Printed in the United States of America

CONTENTS

Title Page
Copyright
Preface
Introduction
Elite
Chapter 1   1
Chapter 2   14
Chapter 3   28
Chapter 4   33
Chapter 5   43
Chapter 6   49
Chapter 7   53
Chapter 8   61
Afterword   71
Acknowledgement   77

PREFACE

How confident do you feel when you stand over a four-footer for birdie or par? When you find yourself 30 or more feet from the hole do you hear a little voice in your head saying, "three-putt territory." These were situations I often struggled with — and saw other golfers struggling with — each time I played.

One day I got a call from my friend Brendon DeVore who I follow on his popular YouTube channel BeBetterGolf. He offered to give me a putting lesson.

When I arrived at the practice green for my putting lesson, I found Brendon waiting for me with golf tees stuck into the green at various points. He told me to hit a few balls to the tees, watching me closely. From the information he gathered he changed my stance slightly and offered some advice about my putting stroke. He also showed me his method of gauging distance and reading greens.

Performance in practice is one thing; performance in competition is something completely different. I needed to test Brendon's teachings on the course. The next day, on the first hole, my approach shot drifted onto the fringe about 40 feet from the hole. The old fear of a three-putt began building. But I used the steps

Brendon showed me to evaluate the distance, read the break, setup and stroke the putt.

I tapped in for par.

While working on this book with Brendon, I continued learning, correcting and refining ways to improve my putting. Gradually, my confidence grew and the dreaded voice that said, "three-putt territory," began to fade. My putting is stonger now than it's ever been.

My hope is that, by reading this book you will learn the steps needed to improve and make putting one of the most enjoyable parts of this wonderful game.

Philip Reed
Long Beach, California

INTRODUCTION

Some years ago, while playing in a tournament, I was facing a 25-footer for par. I was so nervous that I had lost all sense of feel. I literally had no idea how hard to hit the ball. That was because I didn't have a putting system to break the process into steps to cut through the pressure and give me the feel I needed to control distance and accuracy.

Now, after traveling all over the country, interviewing the top golf instructors for my YouTube channel — as well as working with hundreds of golfers like you in golfing boot camps — I've developed the Be Better Golf Putting System. I've taught my system to golfers of all levels and seen them dramatically improve. So
I'm confident that if you read this book and practice these drills it's impossible for you *not* to improve.

Yes, putting is a very individual skill. Let's face it, there are some pretty weird looking putting styles out there. But there are also a few fundamentals that all great putters share. So while there is room for your own variation, what you read here will give you a solid foundation to build your own putting routine on, practice it and take it to the course.

Before we get to the specifics I want to add one more thing. While I'll be recommending some mechanical steps to build your putting routine, I will never rule out the power of the subconscious mind. This is probably the most important element in elite putting, to just let go and trust your sense of feel. Still, that sense of feel is best supported by good mechanics. As you get better at your routine it will become automatic and free up your subconscious mind.

Now, let's get started learning the Be Better Golf Putting System. And get ready to start enjoying the game more and shooting lower scores.

ELITE

PUTTING

CHAPTER 1

The Setup: Build a Solid Foundation

You're reading this book because you want to make more putts. This means making more one-putts and avoiding three-putts. Another way to say that is that you want to hit your long putts close to — or even into — the hole. Once the ball is close to the hole you want to accurately sink your next putt. Clearly, what I'm talking about here is two interrelated skills: distance control and accuracy.

Many golfers think that, because distance control requires a keen sense of feel, it's an inborn quality. You have it, or you don't. But that's not true. You can develop a sense of feel through practice and imagery.

Accuracy, on the other hand, is a bit more mechanical. I'll show you a number of ways to setup up so that you are aligned with the hole and can send the ball on its way home.

So, as we go forward together, remember that we are talking about these two skills — and how to best combine them together to perform under pressure, on the golf course.

Putting-Edge Technology

Before we get to the specifics, let's start with a little tech talk. Using newly developed high-tech putting analysis machines, like the S.A.M. putt lab or CAPTO, researchers have found that the initial line a ball starts on is influenced by three things: the putter's face angle, the path of the putter head, and the location of impact on the club face. Of the three, face angle is far and away the most important factor in starting the golf ball on the right line.

The different factors are broken down in this order of importance:
- 80% by face angle at impact
- 17% by the path of the putter
- 3% by where the ball is hit on the face

Putting is tough and when you are trying to roll a round ball into a small, distant hole everything matters; line, path and strike location — all of it. That being said, nothing determines whether your putt finds the bottom of the cup more than *face angle at impact*. Remember that.

So, a huge part of becoming a good putter is starting the ball on the right line to the hole, which I will refer to as "the start line." Your setup greatly determines your ability to return the face to square at the moment of impact.

To consistently stroke the ball on this start line, it's essential to be stable and motionless from your feet up to the area just above your navel. Unlike a drive that requires great power, a putt only needs an *appropriate* amount of energy and the role of the hips and legs in putting should be to provide great stability.

Accuracy is mainly determined by the angle of the face at impact.

Just as a sharpshooter would not fire his rifle while turning his hips or knees, a great putter like you should create a solid foundation. Being stable and feeling almost planted into the ground will give you confidence that a more simple and reliable mechanism is moving the putter back and through.

Here's kind of a fun mental image for you to keep in mind while setting up for a putt: picture wearing a suit of heavy armor, but just the lower half. If you were dressed in such a thing, you would be immovable from the waist down but your shoulders and arms would be completely free to rock back and through.

To achieve this solid feeling, you will probably want

to have your feet about shoulder width apart and have some bend in your knees. Your feet can be either square to the line of the putt or slightly open. Many great putters, most notably Jack Nicklaus, had an open stance which allowed them to get behind the ball and look down the line of putt.

Your back should be slightly rounded (left) not straight (right), allowing the shoulders to move more freely.

The ball should be either in the middle of your stance or slightly in front of the midpoint. When a ball rests on a green, the weight of the ball makes it sit slightly down, lower than the grass around it. Because of this, the golf ball needs to be slightly lofted out of that depression. That is why putters have between two- and four-degrees of loft built in.

The ball position should help you hit the ball with a stroke that is level or slightly hitting up on the ball. If you hit down on the ball, you will push the ball down into the green causing it to jump. You will constantly be complaining about "bad hops" and be less able to give the ball the appropriate speed.

Keep in mind that the farther forward you move the ball, the more likely you are to strike the ball with a rising stroke. I'll talk more about this later, but when you hit up on the back of the ball, it will cause it to begin rolling more quickly, instead of skidding. Studies have shown that a ball with this so-called "true roll" — rolling end-over-end instead of wobbling on its axis — will hold its line better.

With the ball slightly forward in your stance, it will naturally be struck with a rising stroke and hold its line better.

Addressing A Putt

Now that we've talked about the lower body, you can take your putter and stand over the ball. I like to see your back slightly rounded as you bend to place the putter behind the ball. You can almost imagine that your belt buckle is pointing upwards and your posture resembles a question mark. This stabilizes the lumbar (lower) spine but allows the shoulders (thoracic spine) to rock more freely and consistently when you make the stroke.

You can experiment with these different variables and adjust them as you go. But what's important is to eventually create a setup that puts you in the same position every time. This will provide you with more consistent results.

When it comes to your putting, the only variable should be the length of stroke. Everything else should be consistent. Think of the incomparable Jack Nicklaus hunched over a 60-foot putt for eagle on a random Thursday. Now think of Jack standing over a six-footer for par to win the Masters on a Sunday. You wouldn't be able to tell what putt Jack was hitting just from the setup. His setup would always look the same. Consistency in your setup will also help you eliminate variables so you will know what part of your putting routine you need to work on.

Jack Nicklaus used the same stance, regardless of the distance of the putt.

Try to spend about five minutes a day just practicing

your setup position. Consistently walk into your setup position and get ready to hit a putt. Try to hit a streak of 10 days in a row of practicing your setup for at least a few minutes. Your goal is to make the setup process almost automatic so it will become consistent and repeatable. Then when you're on the golf course, it will feel completely natural and familiar. This will give you the boost of confidence you need to make a putt.

To recap the setup process, here are the basics:

- Build a base that feels solid and eliminates all movement of the lower body
- Feet can be comfortably spaced shoulder width apart
- Toes either square to the line or slightly open
- Feet should aim parallel or left of the start line or slightly open — but never closed
- The ball should be either in the middle of your stance or slightly forward. Avoid putting it back in your stance.

Find A Grip That Works For You

There is nothing more individualized than the putting grip. Turn on a televised golf tournament and you see every variation possible with strange names like the "claw" or the "pencil grip,"

The saw grip can keep the putter face from opening or closing during the stroke. Tiger Woods' grip is shown on the right.

not to mention the popular cross-handed grip. I even remember a tournament where one of the players putted using just one hand. I sometimes think golfers would put a chicken on their heads if it helped them hit the ball in the hole.

These odd grips are for two reasons: trying to get a comfortable, confident, connected feeling and to keep the putter head from flipping open or closed on the backswing.

The purpose of a good putting grip is simple: to return the face to square at impact. Any grip that helps you do that more often is the grip for you. Personally, I like using the left-hand-low grip. It keeps my shoulders level and gives me confidence to control distance and get the ball rolling on my start line.

A Comfortable Grip

Comfort leads to confidence. If you feel comfortable

then you won't fight the putting stroke. So start with the conventional reverse overlap grip (Tiger's grip) and test other grips to see if they feel right for you. Test different grips for yourself. Find a straight 10- to 15-foot putt and see which grip starts the ball on line more often.

I prefer the left-hand-low putting grip.

Remember, some grips don't work equally well for all distances. So test your grip on various length putts: long distance (outside 30 feet) and short (inside six feet), always making sure that putts are *starting on line*. There are ways to control the distance but a good grip should give you great confidence that you can start the ball online from any distance. Maybe you'll discover something that's never been used before. If it works, keep going with it.

Whichever grip you settle on, it's important to hold the putter "lightly, not loosely," master putting instructor David Orr told me. "Tour players hold the putter like a neurosurgeon whereas the average golfer is holding it loosely because they've been told to do that." This can lead to an imprecise, sloppy stroke, says Orr, whose Flatstick Academy is in Southern Pines, North Carolina.

This is one of several tips Orr gave me during a recent interview. Although he works with many pros he said that it's the amateur golfer who can improve the most and the fastest. Learning to read greens and better controlling the speed of the ball are two areas where average golfers will see the most improvement. I'll include his thoughts on greens reading in a later section.

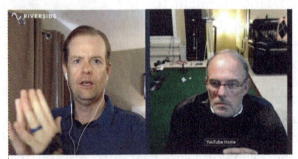

Master putting instructor David Orr (right) speaks with Brendon DeVore in a Be Better Golf interview.

Eliminate Pushing/Pulling

How many times have you heard your playing partners say, "I pushed/pulled that one"? That usually occurs when the putter face is rotated slightly during the backswing. You start square to the target line but as you swing the putter back the face opens or closes slightly and now the ball starts offline. This is particularly noticeable with those dreaded short putts.

This involuntary movement can sometimes be eliminated by using either a pencil or claw grip. The great short game teacher Paul Runyan recommended pressing your elbows into your sides before gripping the putter. As you take your grip, the opposing pressure from your arms will keep the putter head from turning during the stroke.

Once you find a grip that feels comfortable, make sure you place your hands on the putter in exactly the same position every time. This means holding the putter on the same place of the grip each time. I've even seen golfers cut a small notch in their putter grip so, as they slide their hands down the putter grip, they can lock into the same place without even looking.

On my putter I have a small "X" cut into my grip where I place my left thumb. It gives my hands a consistent position and finding that "X" and placing my thumb on it is the start of my routine. Later we will discuss the importance of developing a repeatable routine.

And while we're on the subject of the putting grip, you should explore the different types of grips on the market today. Thicker grips have become popular lately because you can hold them lightly and keep the hands quiet through the putting stroke.

Many golfers like the feel of a tacky grip because it allows a relaxed grip which increases your sense of feel. So if your grip is old, worn and slippery, think about replacing it -- it's an inexpensive investment in your game. Go to your proshop and have them put on a new grip. You'll feel like you just bought a new putter.

Eyes Over The Ball?

Conventional teaching has stressed the need to put your eyes directly above the ball as you set up for a putt. While this seems to make sense it is advice that will only work for a small number of golfers. If you set up with your eyes directly above the ball, when you turn your head to look at the hole, your eyes will play tricks on you. It will look like the hole is really to the left of where it is. This can subconsciously influence your stroke and make you pull your putt.

Instead, put your eyes to the inside of the ball. Now, as you turn your head, the hole will look like where it really is. Knowing this will help you make more putts, particularly those tricky short ones that are so crucial to carding a good score.

To check where your eyes should look when you stand over a putt, put a line on a ball and align it at the hole. Stand over the putt and turn your head to the left. Move your head in and out until the distortion disappears. You might have to move closer in or move back or tilt your head a little. But eventually you

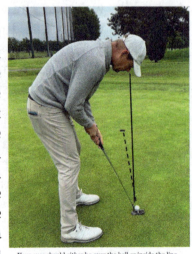

Your eyes should either be over the ball or inside the line.

will find an eye position where the 10-foot straight putt actually looks straight. That's your spot!

Now, make a number of putts this way to prove to yourself that you're lined up correctly. As a golfer and an athlete you are always changing whether you realize it or not. So this process should be repeated every once in a while to check your alignment. If you are putting the ball solid but it is consistently missing, your eye position is the first thing I recommend that you recheck.

PGA player Greg Chalmers, who often had the best putting stats on tour, added two important points. He told me that he uses a mirror to check his eye position. Additionally, he says it's important when standing over a putt, to turn your head in such a way that it keeps both eyes over the line of the putt. This will prevent the line from appearing distorted as you turn your head.

CHAPTER 2

The Putting Stroke

We've now arrived at what most golfers think of as putting: how to swing the club back and through. In fact, the putting stroke is guided -- almost automatically -- by the stable, motionless setup position we talked about in the first chapter. So, what remains is simply moving the putter in such a way to make good contact with the ball and send it on its journey into the hole.

Controlling Distance

There are two ways golfers could control the distance of their putts. The first is that you keep the same length stroke but change the tempo. In other words, you just hit the ball harder. The second method is to keep the same tempo but change the length of the backswing. With a longer backswing the putter head will be moving faster when it strikes the ball causing it to go farther.

The second method, often referred to as a "pendulum motion," is, in my opionion, the superior option. The beauty of this method is that gravity swings the putter head. And, obviously, gravity is a much more consistent force than our own muscles.

The problem with hitting the ball harder, as many golfers do, is that it's difficult to quantify "harder." But with a pendulum stroke, you can quantify "harder" by using a measurably longer backswing.

The pendulum method has a number of other benefits:
- Distance is controlled by the length of backswing
- There is a better chance of striking the ball on the sweet spot
- Under pressure, it gives you a more reliable sense of feel
- It smooths out your stroke on short putts
- It reduces the yips by using the big muscles rather than twitchy hand and wrist muscles

To use the pendulum method, either rock your shoulders or swing your arms from the shoulder joints. The hands do provide a sense of feel by gripping the putter. But during the actual stroke they do little except hold the putter while the bigger muscles do the work. Picture an antique clock with a weighted arm that ticks off the seconds. You can almost hear that calming "tick-tock" sound in your head as you swing the putter back and forth.

It's All In The Wrists

While I just said that the hands do little during the stroke, I should also briefly mention the action of the wrists. If you look back at some of the great putters from the 1960s, and earlier, players used a much wristier stroke with less upper arm motion than today's tour players. If you watch footage of Bobby Locke or a young Gary Player hitting an eight-foot putt, you will see them take a fast, long swing to launch the ball that short distance.

This different putting style was because the greens back then were much slower compared to today's conditions in pro tournaments. Putting today requires *less* launch (to initially lift the ball off the grass) and *less* speed. These changes in greens speed require that we now swing the putter and use the wrist differently than many of the putting heroes in the World Golf Hall of Fame.

That being said, there is an important role for the wrists to play in the putting stroke. The HackMotion sensor is a device that captures data about the movement and angle of the wrist during the putting stroke. HackMotion data show that elite putters don't putt with locked wrists.

The wrists should be firm, yes, but the wrists should have a bit of play in them, especially on mid- and long-range putts. It is this "play," or suppleness, that allows you to make necessary minor adjustments to the amount of force you use to hit the ball.

When putting, you vary your general distance by using the same tempo and adjusting the length of your swing. But to get to tour-level ball speed control you need to have supple wrists.

The wrists aren't locked. They should allow movement for superior distance control.

In this way, if your nervous system unconsciously realizes you took the club too far back, the wrists will give it a little less of a hit. Conversely if your system feels that your backswing was not quite long enough, then your wrists will give the clubhead just a bit more speed. It is an essential move that most players don't realize they are doing but it is crucial to become an elite putter.

Perfect Timing

Physicists will tell you that speed is a function of distance traveled over a certain amount of time. Because you swing the putter at the same tempo, the back and forth will take the same amount of time whether it is a long backswing or a very short one. The longer backswing will, obviously, provide more force and roll the golf ball farther.

To successfully control the distance of your putts, your goal is to establish a stroke that always swings at the same rate. If you swung the putter to the beat of a metronome, it would count at about 75 beats per minute (BPM). You can actually find a metronome on YouTube and bring it with you to the putting green. (But wear earphones so you don't annoy the other golfers.)

Try this drill: With a metronome playing 75 BPM, get maybe 20 golf balls on the fringe of a putting green. Hit putts in a range of different distances, adjusting your length of stroke but keeping the same tempo.

Hit some soft putts only barely onto the green. Hit other putts clear over to the fringe on the other side. And still others to every distance in between. Do this drill with a playful attitude. You are just trying to get your brain to make the realization that the same tempo and different length of stroke is the important factor in controlling the distance your ball travels.

Use a metronome to establish a stroke that swings at the same rate even as your backswing increases.

I'll go into more detail later but it's also a good practice to pace off your putts to get a feel for the distance. You can do this alongside the line of the putt while your partners are lining up their putts. Counting off the distance in 3-foot paces will not only calm you down, by taking your mind off making a crucial putt, but your feet will give you a sense of the green's slope. I'll have much more on greens reading later.

Gaining Strokes On The Field

As you develop your putting routine it helps to have a goal to shoot for. That way you can know what to practice on and how much you are improving.

When I flew to Missipppi to meet with short game expert and PGA professional Tim Yelverton, he gave me a goal for evaluating the distance of your putts.

Yelverton told me to think of getting your lag putts to within 10 percent of the total distance. Of course, if it's only a 10-footer, you will want to get it in the hole or just one foot (10 percent) past. On putts as long as 30 feet you can think of getting it within three feet of the hole except that would be a foot and a half on either side of the cup.

Another way of measuring your progress is to think of the strokes gained system. Here's what will put you ahead of the field:

Short game expert and PGA professional Tim Yelverton says to practice leaving lag putts within 10 percent of the total distance. On a 30 foot putt, that's less than three feet.

- Making half your putts from eight feet

- Always two-putting from 33 feet

Tour players make about half their putts from eight feet (and the surfaces they putt on are nearly perfect). Every time a tour player drains an eight footer, they are gaining half a stroke on the field.

So if you make 50 percent of your putts from eight feet you would be gaining strokes on any field. A distance of 33 feet (which would be 11 paces) is a watershed distance on tour. From *inside* 33 feet, a tour player will one-putt more often than they three-putt. From *outside* 33 feet, a tour player will three-putt more often than they one-putt.

All this means that every time you face a putt 33 feet (11 paces) or longer, two-putting from that distance would gain you strokes on the best players in the world. Too many regular — and even professional golfers — underestimate the challenge of two-putting long putts. Next time you face a putt that is 33 feet or longer, and you're able to get in the cup in two strokes, you should give yourself a pat on the back.

ELITE PUTTING

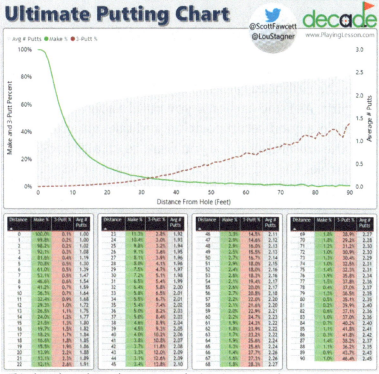

This chart shows that as three-putt rates begin to increase, at about 33 feet from the hole they become more common than one-putts.

You truly deserve it because you would be gaining a fraction of a stroke even on tour players. So, the long and short of it — so to speak — is that if you are able to make half of your eight-footers and two-putt from 33 feet you will be a very good putter.

To see how crucial putting is, try using this cool strokes gained calculator. Track the number and the distance of your strokes and it will tell you how many strokes you've gained on the field.

The Putter's Swing Path

Much has been written about the putting stroke and the path the clubhead takes as it swings back and through the putt. As I said earlier, if you build a solid foundation, stand in a good setup position and take an appropriate (for the amount of force you want to create) backswing the stroke should feel as if it takes care of itself. Your shoulders will move naturally and consistently.

Still, you might be wondering exactly what path the putter head will take. Studies have shown that the most natural motion is a very slight semi-circular path.

In other words, as the putter swings back it will move inside the path slightly. After the putter head strikes the ball, it will then move inside again.

When you use a "straight back and straight through" technique, it actually means you slightly close the face on the backswing and open the face on the through swing. There have

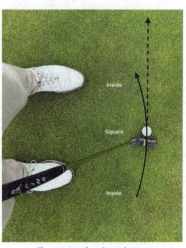

The most natural putting stroke is slightly inside-to-square to inside.

been great putters who advocated a slight "hooding" — or closing — of the putter head as it is taken back. By doing this, the putter can travel straight back and, hopefully, straight through the putt. The only problem is that this technique requires manipulating the putter which adds one more variable.

The more modern style of putting is to simply allow the putter head to swing inside very slightly, square at impact, and then inside after the ball is stroked. The putter head opens and closes relative to the target line but it stays "square to the arc." This is more natural and consistent.

It's important to note that the putter head will be square to the line of the putt well before it reaches the ball and well after striking the ball. The larger the stroke you make the more arc the putter head will have. On very short putts the arc will be almost nonexistent. All I'm saying is that, because of the way your body works, the putter will swing inside-to-square and then square-to-inside. Don't fight it.

To get the feel of the putter head's path, you can use a putting arc that rests on the ground and guides your clubhead on the correct path. There are many such devices on the market. This dual putting arc is perfect for practicing path and is the most popular putting path tool on tour. It can be set at various widths to work with any type of putter. It's well worth the investment to get a putting arc and use it to groove your stroke.

Forward Press

When you stand over a putt you want to make your first

movement back from the ball in a smooth motion that doesn't change the putter face angle. You also want to make sure the putter moves back along the right path. But if you've been standing over a putt, in a frozen, tension-filled posture, the first move you make could jerk the putter offline.

To avoid this, many good putters use a slight forward press: they push their hands forward slightly, then begin the backward motion.

A forward press initiates the backswing more smoothly with a small motion of the wrists.

But I'm not a fan of this move. Mainly, I don't recommend this because, when you make the forward motion, you risk changing the angle of the putter face, either opening or closing it. And having the right face angle is the most important element of putting.

Instead of forward pressing the putter try a "ghost" forward press. Before you take the putter back imagine a slight shifting of weight toward your lead foot, a slight increase in grip pressure and visualize a forward press *without* actually forward pressing. Then rock the putter back. Simply imagining the forward press readies your system for movement so that the motion starts smoothly. This is something that Patrick Cantlay does very well.

I like a smooth, repeating, putting routine that doesn't include a lot of time over the ball. Everything you do in your routine should have a specific purpose and lingering over any part of the routine too much can only hurt you. Less time over the ball makes you more decisive and less prone to having doubt creep into your mind.

Greg Chalmers, two-time PGA Tour leader in strokes gained putting, recently told me it's important to be ready to stroke your putt soon after you get over the ball. "I don't want any surprises when I step into the putt," he says. This means you should have read the green, aligned your ball to the hole and taken a few practice swings. "When I walk into the ball I want to be athletic and go." Once he addresses the ball, he just thinks, "tick-tock, one-two. Bang."

Greg Chalmers, two-time PGA leader in strokes-gained putting.

Hitting The Sweet Spot

Recently, I had the pleasure of interviewing PGA putting expert Bruce Rearick who works with many of the pros. He was very clear about what separated great putters from mediocre or inconsistent putters. He said the great putters hit the ball on the sweet spot of the putter all the time.

You've probably heard this before but to recap, when the ball is hit on the sweet spot of the putter, the force of the putter is efficiently transferred to the golf ball. The ball then rolls the same distance each time. Additionally, the ball will roll on a straight line, despite

hitting bumps in the green, when it has been hit on the sweet spot. If a putt is not hit on the sweet spot it won't go as far and it is more likely to wobble offline.

All this means that, if you can learn to hit the sweet spot, you can begin to build consistency. And, Bruce adds, this consistency will then translate into confidence. As you get the positive feedback by seeing

If you hit your putt on the sweet spot of the putter the line on your ball will roll end-over-end.

your ball roll out to your desired distance, you will begin to trust your feel and your putting will improve.

A good way to train yourself to hit putts on the sweet spot is to put a dot on the putter face's sweet spot with a dry erase marker. Practice putting and try to wear that dry-erase dot off the face of your putter. Similarly, you can also mark the back of a golf ball and try to wear off that mark too.

Distance control is the most important skill in putting, according to Bruce. It's impossible to develop the touch necessary if you aren't hitting the golf ball on the sweet spot. So take the time to find your putter's sweet spot, mark it and hit all your putts on that vital spot.

Putting expert Bruce Rearick (right) says to learn to hit the sweet spot.

CHAPTER 3

Avoiding Three-Putts

I don't like to dwell on the negative side of things, but the sad truth is that three-putting is an occasional part of the game. You could almost say that, at times, three-putting is inevitable. If you look at the reasons that this occurs it helps to avoid it — or at least to move on without beating yourself up about it.

One stat on the PGA tour that always fascinates me is Three-Putt Avoidance. What is so interesting about this stat to me is the amazing degree of expertise some humans can achieve. The following stat is almost unbelievable but it is true.

In 2015 PGA tour pro Freddie Jacobson went an incredible 542 holes in a row without a single three-putt. Unlike ball speed or driver distance, this is a much more attainable stat to keep for regular golfers. I wouldn't expect anyone to go 542 holes in a row without a three-putt but anyone who consistently works on their putting should routinely be able to go two or three rounds without a three-putt. The key is, you want to be *stingy* with your putts, don't spend them foolishly.

An important question to be able to answer when trying to improve your personal Three-Putt Avoidance stat is what is a three-putt? The simple answer is that it's when you are on the green and it takes you three (or more) putts to get it in the hole. But like many things in golf it is not that simple.

All Three-Putts Are Not Equal

Three-putting from 10 feet away is far more damaging to your score than three-putting from 110 feet away, with a double break, going up and over a huge hill and on slick greens. They were both three-putts, true, but the three-putt in the second example was primarily caused because you hit the ball too far from the hole and in a spot that requires incredible touch to get the following shot close to the hole. So when you are tracking three-putts you *really* want to eliminate three-putts from inside 33 feet. Track how many holes you can go without a three-putting from inside 33 feet. If you focus on your process and keep up your training, maybe you will break Freddie's record.

Putting instructor David Orr gave me an interesting list of factors that can lead to a three-putt. By looking it over you might see that it can happen even to the best golfers.

1. **Proximity to the hole.** If you hit your approach too far away from the pin, it could be tough to get down in two. Remember that "33 feet is a magic number" where distance control begins to be critical. Practicing putts longer than 33 feet — which is about 11 paces — will help you gain strokes on the field.
2. **The shape that you are putting over.** If there is a mound between you and the hole, you are left with an "up and over putt" that is difficult. In some cases, you need to die the putt on the backside of the mound and let gravity take it the rest of the way. This makes distance control essential. A putt that has to go up and over a large mound is *much* more difficult than a putt of equal length that is relatively flat. When you have a mound to deal with it you must respect the challenge.
3. **Hole location.** If the pin is placed on a slope the putt becomes much more difficult, particularly if you get above the hole. Also, your second putt on a sloping green means hitting a putt with just the right combination of speed and break.
4. **The "idiot" three-putt.** In this scenario you get a bit too aggressive with the first putt, miss the hole and now have a longer one coming back. Sadly, this can turn a birdie into a nasty bogey.
5. **You're "snake bit."** If you've missed several

short putts earlier in the round, this can leave you "snake bit," says Orr. But keep in mind that the best way to get your round back on track is to make the next putt and keep building your confidence. Your best chance to get back on track is to recommit yourself to focusing on the entire process of hitting your putt. Focus on the process and feel somewhat indifferent to the result and you will bust your slump.

Reviewing this list, I think many golfers will feel they've "been there before." Hopefully, this might help you change your approach to these situations or, at least, help you move on.

Die It In The Hole

The speed of a putt is crucial to whether or not it actually drops into the hole. While a fast putt holds its line better, it makes the target much smaller. To make sure the putt drops it only needs to get over the edge of the hole. The cup is only four and a quarter inches wide. But if the putt is rolling quickly, the target is reduced to about two inches in width. But, because the hole is circular, a dying putt can drop in from any side.

Tiger Woods was famous for hitting short putts so hard they almost bounced off the back of the cup. But this requires supreme confidence in your start line and lots of practice. Find a happy medium for the speed of short putts and try hitting your longer putts so they just drip over the edge of the cup. If you adopt this practice, in the long run, you will make more putts.

Try this drill to improve your confidence and trust in short putts. Set up a ring of eight two-footers around a hole on the practice green.

Dying putts in the hole will enlarge your target, allowing the ball to drop in from any side.

Make each putt into the hole at different speeds. Slam some in on a straight line. Barely creep some in on a high line. And use medium speed for some putts.

This kind of variable practice is very effective training and it will get you to find the speed where you are most comfortable. I like this drill no longer than two-and-a-half feet because your "make" percentage needs to be very high while doing this kind of thing to always be gaining confidence. I wouldn't like to see a golfer practicing hitting six-footers at different, or extreme speeds because a high percentage of them will miss. And it's just not good for your brain to see missed short putts.

CHAPTER 4

Sharpening Your Accuracy

Now, we're going to talk about lining up your putt so you have the best chance of knocking it in the hole.

As I mentioned before, the face angle of the putter at impact is *by far* the most important factor in sending the ball on the proper start line. So the goal of lining up your putt is to align the club face perpendicular to the target line, then swing the putter back and through in a way that will return the putter face dead square at impact.

To simplify this discussion, I'll assume that we have a straight putt of about eight feet. I'm sure that most of you would approach such a putt thinking that it is "makeable." Not to get off track too much, but I like to encourage you to think of every putt as makeable. Still, the chances of making this putt are good and if you do so you will have picked up a half stroke on a tour field, as I mentioned earlier.

All too often, I see my playing partners simply walking up to their ball, bending over and hitting the putt. They have aimed the putt entirely by their own sense of feel. For them, it's a game of hit and hope.

At the very least, it helps to stand behind your ball and look over the top of it toward the hole. In your mind's eye you can draw a straight line between your ball and the hole. This one step helps enormously.

However, as you move from behind the ball to your setup position, there is often a feeling of disorientation. That nice straight line you saw from behind the ball now looks distorted. Doubt creeps in. But you don't want to hold up your foursome so you go ahead and hit the putt anyway. These "anyway" putts are the death of many good rounds of golf.

A much better way to preserve that straight line feeling as you move into your putting setup is to pick a spot in front of your ball, about 10 inches along the path to the hole. Then, keep your eye on that spot as you move into your setup position and align the putter face toward it. Concentrate on rolling the ball over that spot, tracing your eyes up and down from the ball, to the spot and to the hole. If you have the right speed, and the clubhead is square at impact, you will make the putt.

If you've ever gone to a bowling alley, you will see

aiming marks on the lane. This is the same idea. Bowlers will try to roll the ball over one of these marks knowing that the ball will then find the mark.

An even more accurate way to aim your putts is to draw a line on your golf ball using a plastic guide and a Sharpie marker. After picking a spot to roll the ball over, you can then aim the sight line in the direction of your aiming spot, which will be in line with the hole. Now, when you take your setup position, you can be confident that the line is pointing at the hole.

I spent some time being on the fence about using such a prominent line on my golf ball until, on the Golf Channel one day, I heard Nick Faldo say he thought the line on the putting ball should be made illegal. "It helps too much, it really makes it too easy," he said. I was convinced. Using the line really helps, especially eight feet and in.

If there is time before you putt, you can check the accuracy of the line on the ball by using the shaft of your putter as a guide. Aim the sight line on the ball. Then stand behind your putt on an extension of the ball-to-target line and hold your putter shaft up between the ball and the spot you have chosen for your start line. Then, close one eye. If your line is aimed correctly you should see the putter shaft in a perfect parallel match up with the line on the ball.

For a stronger visualization, if it's sunny out, you'll see the sun glaring off a spot on your putter. Tilt the shaft of the putter forward and back so that the glare spot "travels" from the ball through the "spot" and into the hole. This is a powerful way to etch the path of the ball in your mind's eye.

Before you use the sight-line method, try it out on the practice green. At first, you might find that, when you stand over your putt, you think the line isn't really pointing at the hole. If you get this feeling, back off, stand behind the ball and double check it. If you just can't get the line to look right you might need to adjust your eye position (as I described earlier). The key is to trust what your eyes are telling you so you can confidently stroke the putt.

By drawing a line on your ball...

...you can accurately line up your putts, especially those crucial four-footers.

Remember, a golfer that putts confidently to a spot that is slightly wrong will have much more success than a golfer who is still waffling over what the perfect line should be when they stroke the ball. This doesn't mean trying to slam a putt into the back of the hole. Just like hitting a putt too softly, hitting a putt way too hard is also a sign of lack of confidence. It means hitting it confidently and at the *appropriate* speed.

Once you have decided on a line for the putt it's best to remember the words of the American poet and philosopher Henry David Thoreau: "Go confidently in the direction of your dreams. Live the life you imagined." You've imagined yourself as a great putter, go confidently in that direction!

Here's a summary of different ways to aim your putts:
- At the very least, stand behind the ball and draw an imaginary line in your mind that connects the ball with the start line and hole. Keep this line in your mind as you take up your setup position.
- Pick a spot about a foot in front of the ball and keep your eye on it as you take your setup position. Concentrate on rolling the ball over the spot that leads to the hole.
- Draw a sight line on your ball and align it with your aiming spot. Now, when you stand over your putt, there will be no doubt about the path to the hole.

- Stroke it with confidence at the appropriate speed.

Short Putt Strategy

Making your short putts — four feet and closer — is a bit like shooting a free throw in basketball: You know you should make it but you know you'll feel like an idiot if you miss. As you get closer to the hole, your expectations rise. It's almost like the theme song of the movie "Jaws" is playing out of the hole and getting louder and louder the closer you get. And, let's face it, expectations can make a simple task more difficult. It's easy to get tense and try to steer the ball into the hole rather than making a good stroke.

Let me share two stories that separate the mentality and process of golfers who are great at making short putts.

First, take the case of Scott Hoch. In 1989 he had a 24-inch putt to win the Masters. Scott, known for being a good putter, had this short putt to beat Nick Faldo. When you watch the full video of that year's Masters you'll notice that on that putt Scott takes *much* longer in his routine. His routine was getting longer all day and on this crucial two-footer it took Hoch one minute and four seconds from the time he placed the ball down until he stroked the putt. And he missed.

Compare Hoch's missed putt on hole 18 to the putt he made for birdie earlier in the day on the ninth hole. On the ninth hole (from seven feet and a much tougher putt to make than the 24-incher he missed on the eighteenth hole), Scott's time between placing his ball and stroking his putt was exactly 30 seconds. When he had the crucial two-footer to win the Masters his routine took a full 34 seconds longer and on the first playoff hole Faldo won the green jacket.

Years later, when Nick Faldo was doing a television broadcast for a PGA Tour event with his sometimes rival Paul Azinger alongside him in the booth. A tour player missed a very short putt (about the same length that Hoch had missed in 1989) and Azinger was shocked.

"Wow. You expect to make those but that does happen sometimes. I mean if you had to make one thousand two-footers in a row how many would you make?" Paul asked.

"One thousand," Nick replied dryly.

Paul was getting annoyed. "Ok, what about a million. Out of one million two-footers how many would you make?"

"One million. Why would I miss?" Nick insisted.

Obviously if Faldo was to attempt to make one million two-footers, considering the variables of speed, slope and situation, he would probably miss some. However, he would never let that possibility enter his mind. That's how strong his mental game was.

Making short putts is incredibly important. If you are solid on your four-footers, then it allows you to mentally enlarge the area surrounding the hole for your lag putts. And if you make a short putt to save par, you'll walk to the next hole with a boost of confidence.

My opinion is that these short putts are often missed because golfers make too long of a backswing which can get off track. To counteract this tendency, Lee Trevino recommended moving the ball back in your stance, just for short putts. This naturally restricts your backswing and will help keep the putter face aiming at the hole. I believe it's better to err on the side of having a compact backswing rather than a long, possibly loopy backswing. Try a shorter backswing and see if it works for you.

"Aim The Line"

PGA top 20 teaching pro Mike Malaska told me that many amateur golfers over-read the break on short putts. He said to always play the putt inside the hole unless the break is obvious. Then, align the line on your ball and just concentrate on rolling the line. Don't focus on making the putt, focus on the process. Then, roll the line on the ball — and just let the hole get in the way. "Aim the line, roll the line" is a nice thought to have as you get ready to stroke a short putt.

Additionally when it comes to short putts, I've found

that of all the things you can think about during the actual stroke, thinking of hitting the ball on the sweet spot of the putter seems to be the most effective. It quiets your mind, focuses a simple task and reduces doubts.

Mike Malaska, PGA teaching pro, says, "aim the line, roll the line."

To build the right feeling for short putts, here's a drill you can try. Insert a tee about a foot behind your putter on a three-foot putt. Make the stroke without hitting the tee on your backswing. See if you make more putts this way than your normal, longer backswing.

I have several other drills for short putts in the section at the end of this book.

Practice Swings

Before you putt you will probably want to think about the correct length of your backswing. You might be tempted to take a lot of practice swings to dial in the exact length of the backswing. Frankly, I don't think this is particularly productive. Among other things, when you get over the ball, you will find yourself trying to duplicate the backswing rather than just making the correct backswing.

First of all, I don't recommend taking a lot of practice swings. Often, this is nothing more than a stalling tactic used by golfers trying to build the courage to hit a long putt. It's fine to take a few practice swings to get loosened up and groove the right swing path. But don't feel that you need to key in on an ultra-specific backswing length.

Instead, you can use what I call the "Goldilocks Method." Swing the club back just a little and think, "This is too little, this would definitely come up short..." Take a very long backswing and think: "This is too much, this would fly past the hole....". Now you know the correct answer is somewhere between the two. Finally, take a backswing that is somewhere in between and think, "That's just right."

In a sense, you've bracketed the swing you need. But keep in mind that the backswing you use for your actual putt will ultimately be controlled by your subconscious mind based on the look of the distance, slope, green speed and all the other factors in play. Trust that those subconscious factors will work for you.

CHAPTER 5

Reading Greens

When you read the green, your job is to determine which way the ball will turn and whether the putt is uphill or downhill. From these factors you can decide where to aim and how hard to hit the ball.

Reading greens is an area where amateurs could improve their putting the most, says master putting instructor David Orr. As I mentioned earlier, Orr says amateur golfers have lots of room for improvement and can build their skills quickly. Practicing greens-reading will pay dividends next time you tee it up.

A good way to improve your greens-reading skills is to get a slope measuring device, such as a digital level or even a phone app to show the direction and the degree of the slope. Stand on a sloping part of a practice green, guess which way it breaks, and then check to see if you were right. Remember to check the break close to the hole, not farther back.

Obviously, when you're playing, you can't use a level or a phone app. But you can use either the "AimPoint Putting System" or the plumb bobbing method.

The AimPoint Putting System is now being used by a number of pros including golfer Adam Scott. The break is determined by straddling the line of the putt and sensing whether there is more pressure on one foot than the other. You then rate that pressure on a scale of one to five. Finally, stand behind your ball and hold that number of fingers up, aligned with the edge of the hole, to show the starting point of the putt.

After you sense how much slope there is, you can align your fingers to show where to aim your putt.

The plumb bobbing method involves standing behind your ball and lightly holding the putter in front of you so that the putter head is over the ball. Since gravity will always make the putter hang vertically, the slope of the greens will be magnified. You can then look along the shaft to see if it is to one side of the hole or the other.

In both methods, the break is only measured where you are standing, not at a point near the hole which is where the ball will break the most.

If you're old school, you might want to try to measure the break visually. Begin by standing on the low side of the hole which makes it easier to see the contours of the green. It's a little like holding a book as you read it. You hold the book tilted toward you, not away from you. It's the same with reading the greens.

A strong visual image that I often use is to look at the cup and pretend that it is being filled with water. Now, ask yourself where would the water would spill out first? If you picture water flowing out of one side of the cup, then that will tell you where the front door of the putt is. The front door is the point where the ball will drop into the cup.

Once you know which direction the ball will break, you can begin to think about how hard to hit the putt. If there is a lot of break, such as on a downhill putt, you will need less speed and the ball will take longer to reach the cup. An uphill putt will break less and the ball will reach the hole faster.

Remember, as you visualize your putt, the ball will fall in over the high side of the hole. It's better to err on too much break because the ball will always be turning toward the hole. In most cases, if your ball approaches from the low side of the hole it won't fall into the cup.

Visualize the putt rolling across the green and dropping into the cup on the high side of the hole.

A common problem is that golfers see the ball getting to the hole too quickly. As you visualize the putt, watch it in real time as it rolls slowly to the hole and — very importantly — imagine it dropping in. Don't turn off your mental movie too early!

If you simply can't tell which way the putt will break, look around at the green. Does it begin sloping in one direction several feet away from the hole? This could be a clue about which way the ball will turn.

And, of course, it's important to "go to school" on your playing partner's putt if they are on the same line as your ball. Often, a very subtle break is only revealed as their ball finishes its final few rotations. That can make the difference between a holed putt and a lip out.

Another technique for greens reading is to think of which way the water would flow off the green. If there is a water hazard, lake or ocean nearby, the water would probably drain in that direction. Additionally, as the water flows across the grass, it might change the grain, or direction, of the way the grass grows. This will cause the ball to turn in that direction.

Break It Into Thirds

On longer breaking putts, I like to break it into thirds. I begin by reading the third that is closest to the hole since this is where the break will be greatest. This is the "die" section of the putt. And The center third of the putt is simply the "roll" section where the ball will begin to turn in the direction of the slope.

The first third of the putt is the "launch" section where the ball will be moving quickly and the break will have relatively little effect on it.

Read longer putts in thirds and remember the most break will be closest to the hole.

Once you've reviewed each third of the putt, you can determine the start line and speed of the putt. Use the shaft of the putter to align yourself to the spot in line with your aiming point and follow the other steps in your setup routine.

Finally, remember that the most important part of the putt to read isn't where you are standing, it's much closer to the hole. When the ball is rolling quickly, the slope has less effect on the ball. It's really the final few feet, when the ball is dying, that matters. It's that last little bit where the ball will take the break. And, if you're lucky enough to go to school on a playing partner's putt, watch carefully as the ball rolls to a stop. Often, just that last rotation will show you the break.

CHAPTER 6

Putting It All Together

So, those are the pieces of the putting process. Now, I want to share with you a repeatable routine that blends these pieces together into a smooth, efficient routine. Having an established routine will make you more decisive. And being decisive will help you to commit to the shot.

Once you develop a routine that works for you, it's like you are entering a state of flow. You merely go through the different steps, stroke the putt and accept the outcome. I like to tell my students, "It's like the band is playing and you just join the music." Then, you can have peace of mind knowing you gave it your best shot.

I'm going to describe what I do when I'm facing a putt. But I want to encourage you to develop your own routine that fits your temperament and style of putting.

Here are the steps I recommend for making putts:
1. Pace off the putt by walking beside the line from the hole to your ball. Counting the paces will take your mind off the pressure you feel and calm you down. As you walk, use your feet to sense the slope of the green.
2. Read the putt from the low side of the hole. Think of where water could spill out of the cup to see the slope of the green. Look around for other clues — high points on the green or nearby water hazards — to see which way the ball will turn.
3. Now that you know which way the putt will break, if at all, you can stand behind the ball and look toward the hole. Pick a spot about 10 inches in front of your ball along the line of the putt.
4. Align the line on your golf ball so it aims over the spot you've chosen. To check that you are aimed correctly, hold your putter shaft so that the edge of it draws a straight line from the ball to the hole.
5. Stand beside your ball and take two practice swings. You can take more but I recommend always taking a set number of swings. To get the feeling of the pendulum you can think "tick-tock, tick-tock."
6. Move into the solid setup position you have practiced. Take two looks at the hole and then stroke the putt. You can even say to yourself,

"Look... look... go." Using these words keeps negative thoughts from your conscious mind and provides a countdown before you pull the trigger.

I have one other recommendation to offer. That is, I like to approach the putting process with an attitude of gratitude. If you are looking for a "spot" to start your ball and there happens to be one tiny flower in the perfect spot to aim at, think to yourself: "Wow, a flower exactly where I need it! It's a perfect thing to aim for. I'm just lucky." Or maybe your putt is uphill, you can say to yourself: "Great! An uphill putt! I'm really lucky that this ball finished in this position so that I would have an uphill putt."

As you pick an aiming spot in the green, think how lucky you are that it's in just the right place to help you.

Get creative with finding your silver linings. Then get lost in the process and trust your subconscious mind and your sense of feel. You will make more putts. This positive affirmation turns the tables on negativity and will greatly improve your chances of making the putt.

CHAPTER 7

Perfect Practice

Practice is like watering a tree. The water helps the tree grow roots and develop branches and leaves. If you stop watering, the tree eventually dies. Similarly, your putting skills will grow — and continue to grow — with the right kind of practice.

Developing a practice routine, and sticking to it, can help you break 90 for the first time. Or break 80 or even 70. Practice prepares you for a tournament. And practice will help you sharpen the new skills that you just learned.

So much of putting is developing — and then refreshing — that vital sense of feel. And you develop feel by rolling putts and seeing the outcome. Every time you hit a putt, it's like downloading information into your brain's computer's database. The more data you put in, the more accurate it will be. Yes, that process takes some time to show results. Studies have shown that it takes at least 30 days to learn a new skill. So be patient.

Maybe you think you don't have a lot of time to practice. That's okay. You don't have to spend hours on the practice green. In fact, it's much better if you don't. Psycologists say that a few minutes of practice a day is actually better than hours of practice one day a week.

My hope is that you can learn to enjoy practicing. The key is to find a time and place to practice that fits in with your schedule. It's a great idea to have an area at home to sharpen your start-line accuracy. To practice your distance control you might find it relaxing to stop by the putting green on your way home from work.

At Recreation Park Golf Course, in Long Beach, California, where I usually practice, I often see a group of guys on the practice green playing putting games. They're betting against each other, trash talking, laughing and having a great time. And some of them are damn good putters.

Brad Faxon, and many other of the top PGA putters, grew up playing putting games with friends. Not only is it good practice, but it puts pressure on you so you can learn to perform in competition. You don't have to play for a lot of money to feel a surge of adrenaline when you stand over a four-footer to win the match.

Perfect Practice Makes Perfect

Maybe you've heard the expression: "Practice makes perfect." That's only partially true. It really should be: "Perfect practice makes perfect."

What this means is that it's not enough to just knock a few balls around on the putting green. You need to pay attention to the fundamentals described earlier in this book. As you practice, make it really count. Go through your routine each time you face a putt.

If you don't have a friend to compete against, then compete against yourself. See if you can make 10 four-footers in a row. If you have made nine in a row, do you feel pressure to make that last putt? If so, you're beginning to replicate conditions you will face on the course.

And finally, as you conclude a practice session, wait for that moment when you make a nice long putt. When the ball disappears into the hole, stop your practice session with that positive picture in your mind. Never quit on a miss.

Practice At Home

A good system is to set up a practice area at home on your carpet or in your garage. You can buy an inexpensive section of felt and create a small putting green. Mark off different distances, and draw a sight line to the hole, to help your accuracy. Obviously, you won't have these perfect conditions on the course but at least you are proving to yourself that you can roll the ball down the start line.

Without a doubt my favorite way to practice is to put down my cloth-covered yardstick and see how many times I can roll the ball the length of the stick. Seeing the ball start on the right line is a huge boost to my confidence when I go out to play. And it's a sure way to make more of those three- and four-footers.

If you have an analytical nature, you can set up a white board and log your results. See how many four-, five- and six-footers in a row you can make. Keep trying to break your earlier records. After practicing four-footers at home, when you get over a short birdie putt on the course you know just what to do. You can even tell yourself, "I always make these putts at home — this isn't that different."

Stay Out Of The "Dead Zone"

Remember how I talked about trying to make more eight-footers and two-putt from 33 feet? Those are the two areas you want to work on. So break your practice sessions into two sections: lag putting and accuracy putting.

Practicing making 20-footers is what I call
the "dead zone" -- you watch yourself miss repeatedly.

All too often, I see golfers go to the practice green to try to improve, but they have no real system to achieve better results. Instead, they throw down a few balls and try to make 20-footers. There are two problems with this. First of all, a 20-footer is not an especially makeable putt. But it's not a particularly difficult lag putt. So basically, you just watch yourself miss a lot of putts.

Instead, stick a tee in the green, pace off 33 feet (the point at which three-putts begin to increase for pros) and practice rolling the ball to within three feet of the tee. Now, you're not watching yourself miss because, if the ball stops within three feet of the hole, you will have successfully gauged the distance.

Once you've mastered 33 feet, try putting from even longer distances. Pace off 15 steps (45 feet) and even 20 steps (60 feet). You know that eventually you will face putts of this distance — and longer — when you play.

Recently, a student of mine, excitedly told me he had two-putted from 90 feet. And it was up and over a ridge! He explained that he lagged the ball to within about five feet and then made that putt for par. He clearly was successfully combining the two elements of putting — distance control and accuracy.

By practicing from 33 feet you will get out of the dead zone and into the strokes-gained zone.

Say No To Gimmes

How often does one of your playing partners say, "That's good. Pick it up." You might feel a sense of relief. But be realistic. Would you have really made that next putt?

While taking a gimme might speed things up, in the long run, it hurts your game. First of all, you know in your heart that a slippery side hill two-foot putt is missable. Second, this is a chance to really lock down your skills. If you take that little putt seriously, and knock it in the hole, you are improving your skills.

I have a friend who's a professional poker player who loves to gamble on the golf course. He told me that he's learned to beat much better players by never taking gimmes. That's because even good players will miss two- and even one-footers. By getting comfortable holing out every time, he's gained enough strokes on his opponents to win the match — and take their money.

Warming Up Before A Round

Getting ready to play a round of golf is different than practicing. You aren't really trying to build new skills. Instead, you're trying to tune up those skills you've developed already so you will perform under pressure.

With this in mind, here are a few suggestions for an effective pre-round warm up:
- Place a ball so close to the hole you can't miss and knock it in. Now, your brain is programmed to experience the sight, and the wonderful sound, of the ball rattling into the cup.
- Next, lag some putts to the fringe of the green, both uphill and downhill. Don't worry about the accuracy, just the distance. This will give you a feel for distance — and the speed of the greens — without seeing your ball miss the hole.
- Finally, go through your routine and make some short putts. Again, rather than putting at an actual hole, try putting over a dark spot or a leaf on the green. You just want to get a feel for these putts, not make judgments about your skills on that particular day.
- As you move from the practice green to playing your round, don't buy into the negative mindset that infects many golfers. If someone asks how you're putting, enthusiastically answer, "I'm putting great! Thanks!"

Unfortunately, a lot of golfers arrive at the course with little time to warm up. If you have to choose between hitting balls at the range and putting, I'd spend those few minutes rolling the ball. There's nothing more frustrating than having a round filled with missed four-footers and three-putts. Even stroking a few putts to get the feel of the greens will put you ahead of the game. Then, when you stand over your first putt, your senses will be alive and your chances of putting well will improve.

CHAPTER 8

Putting Drills

Here are my favorite drills to reinforce the skills I've described in the preceding chapters. As I mentioned earlier, it's better to practice a little bit every day rather than several hours once a week. Also, remember to track your results and enjoy your practice sessions.

Yardstick Drill

I designed a special yardstick covered in green velvet. To me this is a tool that will become the absolute foundation of anyone's daily routine to improve their putting. As we have seen, a huge part to being successful at putting is *controlling the start line* and *creating a process.* Nothing is better to organically build these skills than the yardstick drill.

Place the yardstick on a level surface and put a ball on the small hole at one end. Challenge yourself to see how long it takes you to get ten in a row to roll off the end of the yardstick. If you miss, start again.

Do this every day for five weeks and you'll see amazing results. Last summer when my nephew, Jack, came out for a visit, we got *very* competitive about who could hit the most putts down the yardstick without falling off one of the sides. One night I was up till 2 a.m. putting and talking with Jack and I made 260 in a row. (I didn't miss number 261, I just had to stop from exhaustion.)

Roll the ball off the end of the yardstick to practice hitting the start line of your putt.

A few days later, Jack and I played golf and we were laughing because we made absolutely *everything* on the course. Since then it has become a staple of my personal putting work and teaching. If you would like a special Be Better Golf felt yardstick, email me contactbebettergolf@gmail.com and I'll send you one.

Building A Feel For Distance

With a metronome or iphone app marking a tempo, get a number of golf balls on the fringe of a putting green. My preferred tempo is 75 BPM but yours may vary. (I just look up 75 BPM on YouTube and play the beat through my phone.) Hit putts of different distances, adjusting your length of stroke but keeping the same 75 BPM tempo. Hit some soft putts only a few feet. Hit other putts clear over to the fringe on the other side. And still others to every distance in between. The tempo is constant and the length of stroke, back and through, is the variable.

Ladder Up And Ladder Down Drill

For *Ladder Up* start by hitting a ball to a tee placed six feet away. Then, hit another ball that must hit or get past your first ball. Your goal is to see how many putts you can hit without leaving one short. Once a ball comes up short of the previous putt, you are out. Do this all the way across the green.

For *Ladder Down* you do the exact opposite. Hit a putt clear across the green trying to come up just short of the edge. Then hit your next ball just short of that. Your goal is to hit as many putts as possible without running one past your previous putt. Go all the way until you reach a tee six feet from you.

These ladder drills were universally recommended to

me by the great putters that I've interviewed and probably the best way to learn instinctive touch.

Short Putt Speed Strategy

Set up a circle of eight 2-footers around a hole on the practice green. Make each putt into the hole at different speeds. Slam some in on a straight line. Barely creep some in on a high line. And use medium speed for some putts. This kind of variable practice will get you to find the speed where you are most comfortable.

Phil's Ring

Phil Mickelson made this circle drill popular after finally breaking through to win his first major.

Measure with your putter shaft to set up a circle of 3-foot putts.

Place eight to 10 tees in a circle around a hole the distance of your putter shaft. (Place the toe of your putter in the hole, lay it down and place the tee at the butt end.) Then try to "complete the circle" both clockwise and counter-clockwise.

Phil would go until he made a hundred in a row but that takes forever and you really need to be on tour quality greens. I recommend doing short sessions more often. If you want more of a challenge, try to complete the circle of eight spots using your 7-iron as your measuring stick.

Try to complete the circle by making all these putts.

One-Putt H-O-R-S-E

Almost without exception every great putter that I have met talks about playing "putting games" maybe for a can of Coke when they were kids. If you can play putting games for a small wager, it is sometimes just as good as an hour spent doing drills.

"Sevens," and 21, are great games but to me One-Putt H-O-R-S-E is the best. The PGA tour stats show that about 8 feet away is the 50/50 make/miss distance. In One-Putt H-O-R-S-E you choose any putt between six and nine feet (two to three paces) and hit it. If it goes in, your opponent has to make it. If he makes it, no letter is added to his HORSE. If he misses it, he gets a letter. When HORSE is spelled, the player is eliminated.

The last guy to make a putt chooses the next location. This game is great because improving your ability to make putts of this distance is where you can separate yourself from other golfers. A golfer who is comfortable, seasoned and excellent at making six- to nine-foot putts is going to be an absolute force on the course.

Hit The Sweet Spot

Set two tees slightly wider than your putter and place the ball right on your putter's sweet spot. As you focus on swinging without hitting the tees, you will automatically hit the ball on the sweet spot of your putter.

Set tees to the width of your putter.

You can also set the tees so that they are at right angles to the line of the putt. Then, as you swing through the gate created by the tees, you will be aligned with the hole. Watch the ball roll when stroked this way. Does it seem to hold its line better without being knocked off track by bumps in the green?

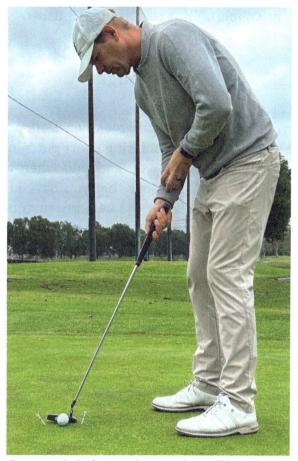

Focus on swinging between the tees and you will hit the ball on the putter's sweet spot.

Short Putt Backswing

Place a tee in the green about a foot behind your ball on a 3-foot putt. Make the stroke without hitting the tee on your backswing. This will keep you from unconsciously making too long of a backswing on short putts which can easily wobble off line resulting in a pushed or pulled short putt.

Final Thoughts

When you watch a golf tournament you will, no doubt, see the pros occasionally missing short putts and even three-putting — just like you and I do when we play. Putting is hard. But the steps that you have just read, which were gathered from the best instructors in the country, will give you a way to systematically approach long lag putts and hole those crucial short putts.

Putting is a skill that needs constant maintenance. You don't need to spend a lot of time on the putting green. But you do need to spend time with focused practice and warm up before a round of golf.

And finally, embrace the challenge of putting. While it isn't easy, it is accessible to everyone. You might not have the strength and clubhead speed of Rory McIlroy or Jon Rahm, but you can putt as well as anyone out there. And if you do, it will bring so much more enjoyment to your game of golf.

ELITE PUTTING

AFTERWORD

By Philip Reed

After reading these pages you might be thinking, "Yes, I really want to improve my putting. But how much better can I really expect to get? And how much time will it take to improve?"

These were the same questions I had as I started this project. After all, putting sometimes seems like black magic — unpredictable and uncontrollable. I think we've all had days on the golf course when we watched, in amazement, as the putts dropped. But then, the next time we played, we couldn't make anything. And it left us wondering what the heck happened.

In golf, more than most other sport, it's hard to see the connection between practice and performance. We might practice chipping, for example, and then the next time we play, we're actually *worse* at it. But if we're patient, the time we spent practicing chipping might help us the next round, or the round after that. By then, though, we've forgotten the time we spent practicing. We're back to just shaking our heads, saying how frustrating and mysterious golf is.

Let me share a little bit of my journey with the flatstick because I think it might help anyone who struggles on the greens.

I took up golf when I was 40 and I knew I'd never be a long drive or first class ball stiker. But I did think that I might become an excellent putter.

This was before the internet and the amazing videos on YouTube (such as those brought to you by Be Better Golf). Instead, I began my putting education by checking out every book on golf I could find from my local library.

My first question was how do you aim your putter so the ball goes in the hole? I assumed there was a method for lining up a putt in such a way that you could hole those "makeable" putts. It soon became evident that there was no universally agreed upon method for aiming putts. Basically, you visualized a line between your ball and the hole and then set your putter head at right angles to that line.

Problem #1: While standing over the ball, your eyes play tricks on you and the line from the ball to the hole appears distorted.

Problem #2: Even if you square your putter face to the line of the putt, when you take it back and swing through, the alignment can change (open or close) and you miss the putt.

Problem #3: You need to hit the putt with enough speed to reach the hole.

Problem #4: If it's a breaking putt, you need to read it correctly, then hit the putt with the right speed to take the break.

So, obviously, there's a lot going on every time you face a putt.

Years ago, I worked with the world's champion free throw shooter, Dr. Tom Amberry, and co-authored the book *Free Throw, 7 Steps to Success on the Free Throw line.* Because of this I began to think of a four-foot putt as a free throw. You really should make it but, as any golfer knows, they can be tough under pressure.

Still, knowing that Dr. Amberry's record was 2,750 free throws in a row, it stretched my mind and made me wonder how good I could become at putting. Initially, I focused on those short putts. But I soon realized that the need for four-footers was often created by not controlling distance well enough.

I experimented with different putters, stances and alignment methods. And, over time, I became a pretty good putter. But, in the back of my mind, I still felt I could get better.

Recently, after nearly 30 years of trying a little of this and a little of that I got a call from Brendon and he offered me a putting lesson. I hesitated because I felt I might lose what ability I had. In other words, I wanted to stay in my comfort zone even though that zone wasn't as good as it could be.

I was pleased to find that Brendon is an excellent teacher. He is very methodical and encouraging. He taught me a system for evaluating putts, reading greens and controlling distance. As he worked with me I said,

"Maybe you should write an ebook about putting." Eventually, we teamed up on the writing project and I fully committed to his methods.

As I worked with Brendon one thing came into sharp focus: controlling distance is the bedrock of putting. I took Brendon's advice and began practicing from 33 feet (the point at which three-putts increase for PGA players) and longer. It was clear that there was no mechanical method for controlling distance — I had to ingrain a sense of feel. Then, when I was on the course, I needed to trust that sense of feel.

Trust, in many ways, was the hardest thing to develop. But after seeing my ability to lag putts to 33 feet (10 paces), 45 feet (15 paces) and 60 feet (20 paces) I became a believer. When I stood over a long putt I just had to tell myself that I had done it before and could do it again. Besides that, having a system to use, and going through the steps, took my mind off the results. As we say in this book, you have to concentrate on the process, not the outcome.

And now for my results. Shortly after finishing the book, and practicing the drills listed here, I had three rounds in the 70s. In those rounds, I had no three-putts, despite the fact that one putt was nearly 90 feet! And I made all my short putts.

How much did I practice? Well, I'm lucky to live near a golf course so I can easily drop in for a short practice session. Also, I have a place in my garage where I practice four-footers. But the amount of practice I did was similar to what anyone else can do — anyone, that is, who is really interested in improving.

There is no magic formula to achieve elite putting. It will take practice and dedication. But the results will be worth it. I know they were for me. And I look forward to still improving even further.

I hope what you've read in this book will encourage you to expand your mental concept of your abilities. Because, as a good friend of mine once said, "We are more limited by our beliefs than our abilities."

ACKNOWLEDGEMENT

This book would not have been possible without the information and support of many awesome golf instructors. I encourage you to seek them out and learn directly from them. I'd like to thank Tim Yelverton, Mike Malaska, Tony Luczak, Tim Tucker, Greg Chalmers, David Orr, Bruce Rearick, Guerin Rife and more.

I'd also like to thank my amazing wife Carmen for her support and love.

About The Authors

Brendon DeVore is the creator, producer and host of one of YouTube's top golf instruction channels "Be Better Golf" with over 140,000 subscribers and 30 million views. Brendon has interviewed some of the most influential and interesting voices in golf instruction while tracking his own progress to be better. He has been an assistant coach for high school and college golf programs and has run dozens of Be Better Golf schools around the country teaching hundreds of students of all ages and abilities.

Originally from Philadelphia, Brendon graduated from

Temple University with a degree in film and media arts and works as a television producer and editor. He lives with his family in Long Beach, California and is a scratch golfer.

Philip Reed is the author of a dozen fiction and nonfiction books including the cult classic *In Search of the Greatest Golf Swing, Chasing the Legend of Mike Austin.* Philip's other nonfiction books are about free-throw shooting and becoming a blackjack card counter. His novel *Bird Dog* was nominated for the top two mystery awards and has been optioned for a movie. He is currently a nine handicap and with Brendon's help he hopes to soon shoot his age.

Made in the USA
Coppell, TX
21 August 2023